Adrenaline Adventure

Leading the Pack:
Dogsled Racing

Jeff C. Young
ABDO Publishing Company

visit us at
www.abdopublishing.com

Published by ABDO Publishing Company, 8000 West 78th Street, Edina, Minnesota 55439. Copyright © 2011 by Abdo Consulting Group, Inc. International copyrights reserved in all countries. No part of this book may be reproduced in any form without written permission from the publisher. The Checkerboard Library™ is a trademark and logo of ABDO Publishing Company.

Printed in the United States of America, North Mankato, Minnesota.
092010
012011

 PRINTED ON RECYCLED PAPER

Cover Photo: Photolibrary
Interior Photos: Alamy pp. 18, 29; AP Images pp. 12, 20; Corbis pp. 1, 6–7, 14, 16–17, 24–25, 26; Getty Images pp. 5, 20–21, 27; iStockphoto pp. 9, 11; National Geographic Stock p. 31; Photolibrary pp. 22–23

Series Coordinator: Heidi M.D. Elston
Editors: Heidi M.D. Elston, Megan M. Gunderson
Art Direction & Cover Design: Neil Klinepier

Library of Congress Cataloging-in-Publication Data

Young, Jeff C., 1948-
  Leading the pack : dogsled racing / Jeff C. Young.
     p. cm. -- (Adrenaline adventure)
  ISBN 978-1-61613-549-2
  1. Sled dog racing--Juvenile literature. I. Title.
  SF440.15.Y685 2011
  798.8'3--dc22
                                     2010028244

Contents

Early Racing 4
Racing Types 6
Sled Dogs 8
The Sled 10
Mushing Gear 14
Training the Team 18
Race Rules 22
Famous Mushers 26
Where to Race 28
Glossary 30
Web Sites 31
Index 32

Early Racing

Long before snowmobiles and airplanes, people used sled dogs for transportation. They were vital to people living in arctic regions. Sled dogs hauled cargo and people through deep snow. They were especially useful for getting mail and medicine to hard-to-reach places. Eventually, humans began using sled dogs for recreation.

Dogsled racing in Alaska began in 1908. This first race was called the All Alaska Sweepstakes. It is still held today. The course runs from Nome to Candle and back. That is a distance of 408 miles (657 km). In 1908, the winning driver was John Hegness. His time was 119 hours, 15 minutes, and 12 seconds.

Interest in dogsled racing spread throughout North America. The first race in the **continental** United States was the American Dog Derby. It was held in 1917 in Ashton, Idaho. The course ran for 55 miles (89 km).

Today, dogsled racing is a tradition in many areas of the world. The International Sled Dog Racing Association (ISDRA) is the major dogsled racing organization. It promotes the sport and enforces rules. There are ISDRA members in countries such as Sweden, Canada, and even Jamaica. They all fight to lead the pack!

Today, most sled dog teams are used for racing or recreation.

Racing Types

Like automobile racing, dogsled racing has different types of competitions. All races use a sled, a dog team, and a driver who's called a musher. The three types of **endurance** racing are sprint races, mid-distance races, and long-distance races.

Sprint races are the shortest form. They are up to 30 miles (50 km) long. Mid-distance races range between 50 and 200 miles (80 and 320 km). They usually begin and end on the same day. Long-distance races run between 200 and 1,000 miles (320 and 1,600 km) or more.

Usually, teams start at intervals rather than all at once.

In that way, they are competing against the clock. The team that covers the course in the shortest time is declared the winner.

Other sled dog events include weight pulls and freight races. For weight pulls, dogs try to pull the most weight. In freight races, a sled is loaded down with a specified weight load. The load is based on the number of dogs on the team. The dogs try to pull their sled faster than the other teams.

IDITAROD

Alaska's annual Iditarod Trail Sled Dog Race has become the world's best-known dogsled race. It runs from Anchorage to Nome. This famous race was first held in 1973.

In 1925, part of the current Iditarod Trail became a route for transporting emergency medicine to Nome. The successful mission helped protect Nome from a diphtheria epidemic. Today's Iditarod race commemorates that 1925 event.

Over the years, the length and the route of the Iditarod have varied. But, the grueling race is roughly 1,100 miles (1,770 km) long. Teams consist of 12 to 16 dogs. Mushers complete the course in 10 to 17 days.

Sled Dogs

The most important part of dogsled racing is the dogs! Sled dogs aren't limited to any one breed. Any dog with the desire to pull and please can be a sled dog.

Both purebred and crossbred dogs compete in the sport. The Alaskan malamute, the Siberian husky, and the Samoyed are common purebreds. Recently, German shorthairs and English pointers have been crossbred with Alaskan huskies. These new dogs are setting sprint race records!

A dog team has some of the same basic needs as any other sports team. These include a proper diet, top-notch health care, and regular practice and exercise.

The challenges of racing mean the dogs eat a lot. In summer when they are not competing, sled dogs consume around 800 calories a day. But during a long, cold winter race, they need up to 10,000 calories daily!

Unlike humans, sled dogs require a diet high in fats and protein. Fats provide quick energy. Protein helps the dogs withstand the physical demands of racing.

During the Iditarod, one dog team eats about 2,000 pounds (900 kg) of food!

Water is considered the most important part of a sled dog's diet. Dogs cannot get enough water by eating snow. It takes a lot of energy to melt the snow. And, a large amount of melted snow creates only a small amount of water. So, it is important that there is fresh water available for the dogs.

The Sled

Whether for racing or transportation, each dogsled has the same basic design. The sled is built upon a pair of skis called runners. Originally, runners were usually made of wood. However, most modern runners are made of aluminum. They have a plastic coating on the bottom. This slick surface reduces drag that would otherwise slow down the sled.

The sled's cargo bed carries equipment and supplies for the team and the musher. It can also be used for transporting a sickly or injured dog.

The brushbow on the front of the sled is like a bumper on the front of a car. It **deflects** tree branches and brush. It also provides protection if the sled collides with another object. Most modern sleds have a plastic, triangle-shaped brushbow. To maintain balance when racing, the musher grips the handlebar.

Footboards give the musher something to stand on while the sled is moving. They are usually made of rubber or another material that prevents slipping. The footboards are mounted on the back of the runners.

Successful mushers move speedily along the trail. They rely on a combination of braking, leaning, and well-trained wheel dogs.

    The brake is located between the footboards. It is a U-shaped bar made of steel or aluminum. Two metal claws hang from it. When the musher stands on the brake, the claws dig into the snow. This stops the sled.

    The track, or drag, is a rubber mat located between the footboards. It acts as a second brake. The mat drags over the top of the ground to slow down the team.

The snow hook is like an anchor on a boat. It keeps the sled from moving after it has been stopped. The team may try to pull when the snow hook is engaged. But, this just drives the hook deeper into the snow.

The snubline is simply a rope. The musher uses it to tie up the sled during breaks or extended stops. Most snublines have a quick-release snap. This keeps the musher from having to tie and untie knots to secure and release the sled.

A well-built and well-maintained sled will glide easily over a flat, straight trail. But, the sled doesn't have a steering system for getting through turns and corners. The mushers get through those course conditions by leaning from side to side. It's similar to what a downhill skier does.

The track and brake also help the musher control and steer the sled. Using them at the right time aids in making tight corners. If they're not used, the sled will swing toward the outside of the corner.

Mushing Gear

During the Iditarod, one sled team may use as many as 2,000 booties!

Almost all sports have their own special equipment. Dogsled racing is no different. Most of the equipment is used to secure the dogs to the sled. It helps provide safety and comfort for the team.

A gangline connects the dogs to the front of the sled. It runs between paired dogs. Along with the gangline, each dog is strapped into a harness. The harness fits across the dog's shoulders, chest, and back. A tugline runs from the back of each harness to the gangline. A neckline attaches each dog's collar to the gangline. It prevents the dogs from veering off left or right.

Sled dogs are hardy creatures. Still, they need protective clothing for their paws. Booties protect the paws from injuries. They are vital. A dog with an injured paw will slow down the whole team.

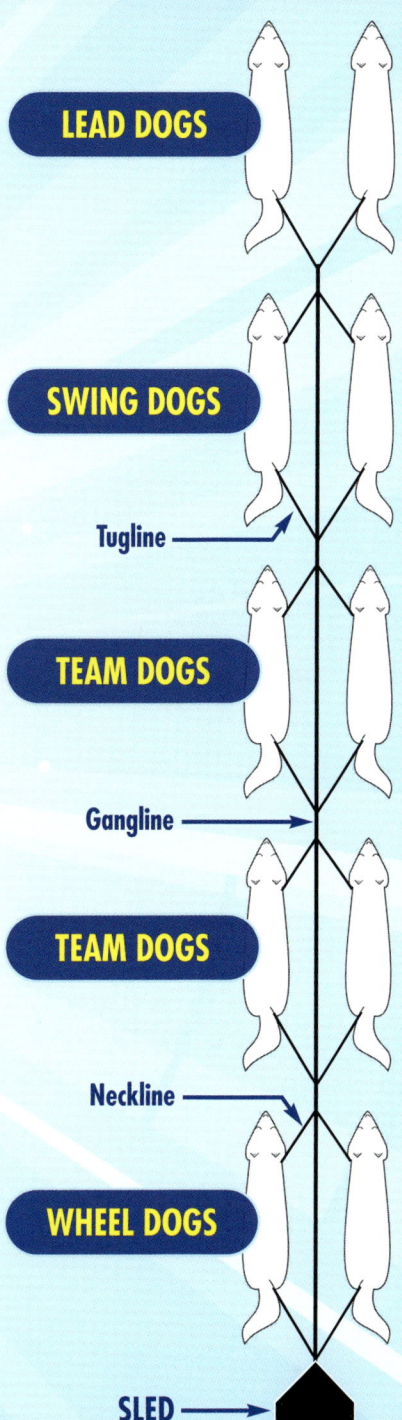

A SLED DOG TEAM

Each member of a dogsled team has an important role to play.

The lead dogs are eager and willing to run in the front of the team. They find the trail and set the pace. Most important, they understand and listen to their musher's commands.

Swing dogs help the lead dogs set the pace. They also assist in turning the team.

Team dogs simply follow the dogs in front of them and pull.

Usually, wheel dogs are the largest dogs. They help their driver keep the sled on the trail. The wheel dogs are important in helping the musher control the sled, too.

Long-distance races such as the Iditarod have special equipment requirements. This includes an ax, a pair of snowshoes, and a cold-weather sleeping bag. The Iditarod also requires a set of eight booties for each dog.

Races can continue through stormy weather or dark nights. So, it is recommended that each musher wear a headlamp. The lead dogs should also wear a light. Reflective clothing such as vests will make mushers and dogs more visible. Dogs should also be outfitted with lighted collars and reflective lines. Reflective tape on the sleds and harnesses also makes the racers easier to see.

Sled dogs are transported to races in special trailers.

The use of layered clothing keeps the mushers reasonably warm. It also protects them from stinging winds and **frostbite**. The first layer of clothing consists of polypropylene long underwear and socks. Polypropylene won't absorb moisture. Heavyweight fleece clothing is the second layer of protection. The third layer is some type of wind-resistant GORE-TEX.

During extremely cold or stormy conditions, a fourth layer is used for protection. That layer is a heavy parka or snowsuit. A musher may cover all those layers with a light wind anorak. This jacket keeps the bone-chilling winds from whistling through zipper cracks.

Before snow falls, mushers start training on dry land.

Training the Team

All dogsled racing begins with training a team of dogs to work together. The training begins when they are still puppies. The musher begins bonding with the pups by handling them and playing with them.

At two months old, a pup starts wearing a collar and a harness. As the pup gets older, a weighted object is attached to the harness. This helps the pup get used to hauling weight. The musher also begins teaching the pup basic sled dog commands.

After learning the commands, the pups are ready to start training as a team. That occurs when they're between six and eight months old. For their first outing, they may have an experienced lead dog to guide them. They begin with short runs and light loads. Then, the runs get longer and the loads get heavier. Slowly, the dogs build up their **endurance** and strength.

LINGO

DOG IN BASKET – a dog riding in the sled because of injury or fatigue.

DROPPED DOG – a dog that has been removed from the race and left at a checkpoint by the musher.

"EASY" – tells the team to slow down.

"GEE" – tells the team to turn right.

"HAW" – tells the team to turn left.

"LET'S GO," "HIKE," OR "ALL RIGHT" – commands to get the team started.

"LINE OUT" – a command to straighten the team out and tighten the gangline. This command is used when the team is stopped.

"ON BY" – a command to tell the team to ignore a distraction on the trail.

STOVE UP – a musher or a dog that is injured.

"TRAIL" – used to request the right-of-way on the trail.

"WHOA" – a command to tell the dogs to stop.

You don't need special certification to become a musher. You just need the proper equipment and a dog team. It is important to have a strong competitive spirit. A love of the sport and the outdoors are also needed. Of course, you should also love dogs! And, you need the knowledge to make necessary repairs to your sled.

Dogsled drivers need the strength to control their teams and **endurance** for competing. People of any size or weight can become mushers. But, it is important to be in good physical condition. A musher often has to help push a sled up a steep slope or through an obstacle. Sometimes, the musher even has to move a sled when it overturns.

Besides being fun, dogsled racing can serve as a stress reducer. The challenge of competing and the enjoyment of being around other racing fans can lift your spirits. All of this can improve your physical well-being, too.

Many mushers consider their dogs family.

A successful musher has to do several jobs. On the trail, a musher becomes a veterinarian, a cheerleader, a mechanic, and a navigator. If you love being outdoors and competing, you won't mind the work!

Race Rules

After all that training, you and your team will be ready to race! For each event, a team of judges enforces the rules of the race. Officials look for illegal equipment or unsportsmanlike conduct. The race marshal is in charge of the race. If he or she determines that a dog team is physically unfit to compete, it can be **disqualified**.

At least one veterinarian is on call during a race. The veterinarian will disqualify a team that has a dog with a disease that is catching.

In a long **endurance** race, veterinarians are stationed at checkpoints throughout the course. They examine each dog and record the results in a book. The musher must present the book at the next checkpoint. Mushers also closely monitor their dogs for warning signs of an injury.

Many of the ISDRA's rules are designed to protect the sled dogs. Physical abuse of the dogs is forbidden. Any musher convicted of animal abuse or neglect will be barred from the race.

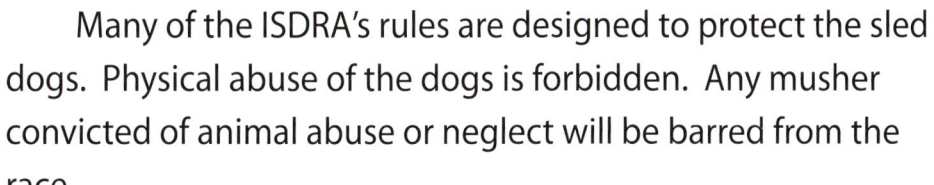

A driver is not allowed to strike a dog with anything, including a whip.

Giving a dog any kind of performance-enhancing drug is also forbidden. That includes anything from aspirin to steroids. Choke collars, **muzzles**, or other devices that could harm dogs are also banned.

Substituting one dog for another is illegal. So, dogs are implanted with microchips to keep track of them. The microchips are checked at the start of the race. That prevents the use of substitute dogs.

Teams must stay on the marked trail throughout the race. There may be unknown **hazards** off the trail. So, taking a shortcut can be dangerous.

An ISDRA racecourse must follow certain rules and regulations. These include keeping the trail free of hazards such as fallen trees and unmarked ruts and bumps. And, the distances along the trail have to be correctly stated.

Sled dog racing also has rules of the road. Teams have to observe the right-of-way and yield it to other competitors. And, they must follow rules on when and how one sled can pass another. Showing a reckless disregard for the safety of others can result in **disqualification**.

Some sled dog racing clubs have their own rules. However, mushers are always expected to practice good sportsmanship. And, they must treat their dogs kindly. Mushers who consistently and willfully break rules can be disqualified from a race. In extreme cases, they can even be banned from future competitions.

Famous Mushers

Dogsled racing may not be as popular as other sports. Still, there are many well-known mushers. Martin Buser and Jeff King are two of the best-known male mushers. They are both four-time winners of the Iditarod. In 2002, Buser became the record holder for the Iditarod. Buser and his team finished in 8 days, 22 hours, 46 minutes, and 2 seconds!

Montana native Doug Swingley is also a four-time Iditarod champion. In 1995, he became the first racer from outside Alaska to win the race. Rick Swenson has won the Iditarod five times. He holds the record for the most wins.

Rick Swenson

Susan Butcher

In 1985, Libby Riddles became the first woman to win the Iditarod. Susan Butcher is the female with the most Iditarod wins. Butcher won the prestigious race four times before her death in 2006. Today, Alaskans celebrate Susan Butcher Day on the first Saturday in March.

Where to Race

Some dogsled races take place on dry land. But, most racing is done in places with cold winters and ample snowfall. In the United States, dogsled racing is popular in Alaska, Minnesota, Michigan, Montana, and New Hampshire. The sport has also found followers in Canada, Sweden, Norway, Germany, and France.

The Iditarod is regarded as the **premier** dogsled race. However, many other races have attracted a sizable following. The Yukon Quest Race runs from Fairbanks, Alaska, to Whitehorse, Canada. This is a distance of 1,000 miles (1,600 km).

Alaska's Copper Basin 300 is a mid-distance race. The Laconia World Championship Sled Dog Derby in New Hampshire is a series of race events. It includes junior races. In Minnesota, the John Beargrease Sled Dog Marathon is held each year. Teams travel along nearly 400 miles (640 km) of Lake Superior's North Shore.

The best way to get started in dogsled racing is to join a club. You will meet experienced mushers and learn about the sport. You can find out if there's a club in your area by contacting the ISDRA.

Some clubs have junior dogsled races. This will give you the opportunity to develop your skills. With enough practice, your team will soon be leading the pack!

Most races are run along back roads or trails.

Glossary

continental - being part of the lower 48 United States.

deflect - to turn something aside from a fixed or straight path.

disqualify - to bar from competition or from winning a prize or a contest.

endurance - the ability to sustain a long, stressful effort or activity.

frostbite - the freezing of the tissues of a body part, such as a hand.

hazard - a source of danger.

muzzle - a fastening or covering for an animal's mouth to keep it from biting or eating.

premier - first in rank, position, or importance.

Web Sites

To learn more about dogsled racing, visit ABDO Publishing Company online. Web sites about dogsled racing are featured on our Book Links page. These links are routinely monitored and updated to provide the most current information available.

www.abdopublishing.com

Index

A
ax 16

B
booties 15, 16
breeds 8
Buser, Martin 26
Butcher, Susan 27

C
Canada 4, 28
clothing 16, 17
collar 15, 16, 19
competitions 4, 6, 7, 8, 10, 16, 18, 20, 21, 22, 23, 24, 25, 26, 27, 28, 29

D
dogs 4, 6, 7, 8, 9, 10, 12, 13, 14, 15, 16, 18, 19, 20, 22, 23, 24, 25, 26, 28, 29

F
France 28

G
gangline 14, 15
Germany 28

H
harness 15, 16, 19
headlamp 16
Hegness, John 4
history 4

I
International Sled Dog Racing Association 4, 23, 28

J
Jamaica 4

K
King, Jeff 26

M
mushers 6, 10, 12, 13, 16, 17, 18, 19, 20, 21, 22, 23, 25, 26, 27, 28

N
neckline 15
Norway 28

R
Riddles, Libby 27

S
safety 10, 14, 15, 16, 17, 22, 23, 24, 25
sled 6, 7, 10, 12, 13, 14, 15, 16, 20, 25
sleeping bag 16
snowshoes 16
Sweden 4, 28
Swenson, Rick 26
Swingley, Doug 26

T
training 8, 18, 19, 22, 29
tugline 15

U
United States 4, 26, 27, 28

32